# true serenity

finding peace in a hectic world

TRUE SERENITY

Summersdale Publishers Ltd
46 West Street
Chichester
West Sussex
PO19 1RP
UK

www.summersdale.com

Printed and bound by Tien Wah Press, Singapore

All images © Shutterstock

ISBN: 1-84024-587-5
ISBN 13: 978-1-84024-587-5

# true serenity

finding peace in a hectic world

alastair williams

summersdale

## Acknowledgements

Alastair would like to thank Lucy York for all her help and input into the book, and Rob Smith for his design work.

The poor long for riches, the rich long for heaven, but the wise long for a state of tranquillity.

Swami Rama

Run a warm, scented bath, have some classical music playing softly in the background, light some aromatherapy candles, pour yourself a glass of wine or freshly squeezed juice, slide into the water and... relax.

There is a serene
and settled majesty
to woodland scenery
that enters into the
soul and delights
and elevates it, and
fills it with noble
inclinations.

**Washington Irving**

Put freshly laundered and ironed sheets on your bed and sink into a blissful cocoon of restfulness.

There are places and
moments in which one
is so completely alone
that one sees the world
entire.

Jules Renard

Steal a moment of silence in your day. Go somewhere you can be alone and block out background noise with earplugs. When silent, listen to your heart beating, the sound of your own breathing, and focus on just existing.

If you live near the sea, go there in the winter when there are no crowds, and just listen to the sounds and rhythms of the sea and breathe in the salty air.

Everything you do can be done better from a place of relaxation.

Stephen C. Paul

Sit in front of a real
fire with the lights
off and listen to
the crackle of wood
burning.

Go for a midnight walk or an early morning stroll. At these quiet times, when no one else is around, you will have the chance to notice things you look past every day.

There is no greatness where there is not simplicity.

Leo Tolstoy

When it's pouring with rain, find a quiet spot and sit in your car. Listen to the sound of raindrops pattering against the roof and windows.

Take a morning walk barefoot across the lawn and feel the dew on the grass beneath your feet.

He who lives in harmony with himself lives in harmony with the world.

Marcus Aurelius

Sit on a park
bench and just
watch the world
go by.

Take time out to be still, withdraw from the life going on around you and find somewhere special to enjoy the view.

He who would be serene
and pure needs but one
thing; detachment.

Meister Eckhart

Fill your room with the subtle scent of herbs and spices to soothe your senses. If you don't have an oil burner, fill a small bowl with hot water and some fresh lavender and place it on top of your radiator.

Bake some bread. Channel any tension into kneading and pummelling the dough, then sit back and inhale as the wonderful aroma of freshly baked bread fills the room.

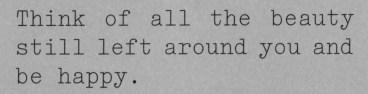

Think of all the beauty
still left around you and
be happy.

Anne Frank

Go cloud watching.

De-clutter your life; chuck out all that useless junk and set aside things you don't really use to give away to someone else who might. It will make you consider the more important things in life.

The time to relax
is when you don't
have time for it.

Sydney J. Harris

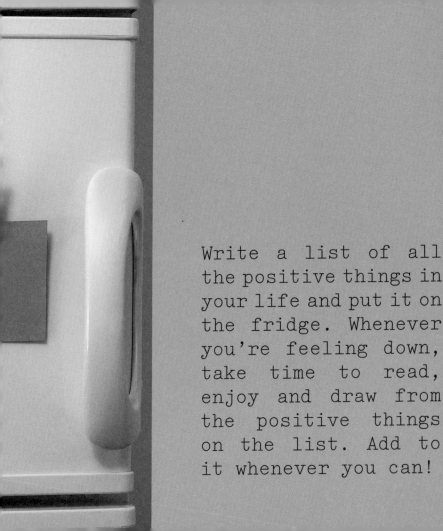

Write a list of all the positive things in your life and put it on the fridge. Whenever you're feeling down, take time to read, enjoy and draw from the positive things on the list. Add to it whenever you can!

You cannot perceive beauty,
but with a serene mind.

Henry David Thoreau

Switch off the TV and spend time alone doing whatever it is that relaxes you, whether it's curling up with a good book, doing a puzzle or writing a letter to someone you haven't been in touch with for a long time.

In the summer, don't
have your lunch in the
office; take a sandwich
to a nearby park.

The more tranquil a man becomes,
the greater is his success, his
influence, his power for good.
Calmness of mind is one of the
most beautiful jewels of wisdom.

James Allen

Skim stones across the unbroken surface of a calm lake.

Spend some time in the library reading or just flicking through magazines and old books. Tune in to the atmosphere of quiet and listen to the sounds of pages turning and people concentrating around you.

Learn to get in touch with
the silence within yourself
and know that everything in
life has a purpose.

Elizabeth Kübler-Ross

Sit in a church. Even if you don't normally go to church, you will find it a peaceful place where you can reflect and gather your thoughts.

Go for a swim and enjoy the sensation of being underwater; the water against your skin, the feeling of weightlessness, the muted sounds...

Peace comes from
within. Do not seek
it without.

Gautama Siddharta

Next time it snows, go outside and watch the snowflakes floating softly down from the sky. Experience the special silence that only snow can bring, and be the first to make footprints on an unblemished blanket of snow.

Take a step back
in time to your
youth; watch one
of your favourite
childhood movies
or go somewhere
that brings back
happy memories.

Adopt the pace of
nature: her secret
is patience.

Ralph Waldo Emerson

Spend time relaxing
with old friends,
sharing memories
and catching up.

Go to bed early in your pyjamas, after massaging your feet with cream and putting on some soft socks.

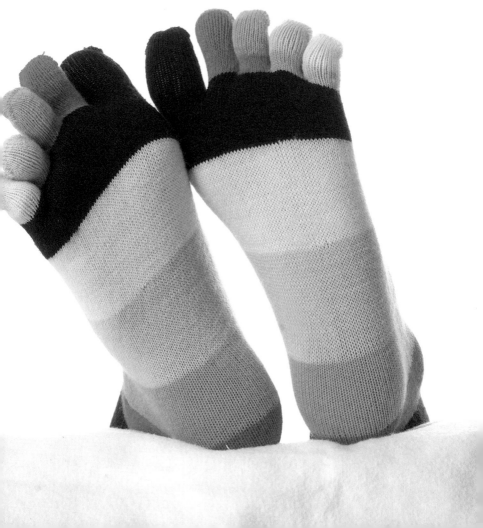

There is time for everything.

Thomas Edison

Have a reassuring
cuddle with someone
you are close to.

At the weekend, have an extra long lie in. Have breakfast in bed, read the newspaper and just relish the feeling that you don't have to get up and go anywhere unless you feel like it.

We must not allow the clock and the calendar to blind us to the fact that each moment of life is a miracle and mystery.

H. G. Wells

Rest is not idleness, and to lie sometimes on the grass on a summer day listening to the murmur of water, or watching the clouds float across the sky, is hardly a waste of time.

Sir John Lubbock

Isabel Losada

100

Reasons
to be glad

# 100 Reasons to be Glad

Isabel Losada

£4.99 hardback

ISBN-10: 1 84024 548 4
ISBN-13: 978 1 84024 548 6

This gently profound gift book celebrates the simple joys in life. From the bizarre to the sublime, there's a lot to be glad about:

*The chance to smile at strangers... Wild poppies... Cats choose to live with human beings... Tantric sex.*

Isabel Losada is the internationally acclaimed author of *The Battersea Park Road to Enlightenment*.

www.summersdale.com